MASTER YOUR INNER WORLD

BONUS GIFT

Get your free ebook and try out our newsletter here:

www.soundwisdom.com/classics

THANK YOU FOR
PURCHASING THIS BOOK!

OTHER SOUND WISDOM BOOKS
BY EARL NIGHTINGALE

The Strangest Secret

Lead the Field

Successful Living in a Changing World

Transformational Living: Positivity, Mindset, and Persistence

Your Success Starts Here: Purpose and Personal Initiative

Your Greatest Asset: Creative Vision and Empowered Communication

The Direct Line

MASTER YOUR INNER WORLD

OVERCOME NEGATIVE EMOTIONS,
EMBRACE HAPPINESS,
AND MAXIMIZE YOUR POTENTIAL

EARL NIGHTINGALE

Published and distributed by:

SOUND WISDOM

P.O. Box 310

Shippensburg, PA 17257-0310

717-530-2122

info@soundwisdom.com

www.soundwisdom.com

While efforts have been made to verify information contained in this publication, neither the author nor the publisher assumes any responsibility for errors, inaccuracies, or omissions. While this publication is chock-full of useful, practical information; it is not intended to be legal or accounting advice. All readers are advised to seek competent lawyers and accountants to follow laws and regulations that may apply to specific situations. The reader of this publication assumes responsibility for the use of the information. The author and publisher assume no responsibility or liability whatsoever on the behalf of the reader of this publication.

ISBN 13 TP: 978-1-64095-499-1

ISBN 13 eBook: 978-1-64095-500-4

For Worldwide Distribution, Printed in the U.S.A.

1 2 3 4 5 6 7 8 / 28 27 26 25 24

CONTENTS

CONTENTS

SELF-ACTUALIZATION AND OTHER LIFE REMEDIES

Have you given much thought to the fact that you create yourself? You do, to an altogether unsuspected extent, simply by the choices you make—by the things you decide to do or not do.

As Kierkegaard said, "The self is only that which it is in the process of becoming." So it is that an adult can stand in front of a full-length mirror and take a good look at what he's created.

We leave home, and we form ourselves into new people; and we learn, as Thomas Wolfe learned, that we can't go home again, that we don't fit as well as we used to. We wonder, after a visit, as we leave to regain our lives, what happened; if something is wrong, what the strangeness was. It is simply that we are different now, and going back

Listen to your inner voice and try to make decisions that tend to be growth-oriented.

home again is like trying to get a two-year-old shoe on a teenager. It's not going to fit anymore.

We have shaped ourselves into new people. And we have done so by our own decisions. There's no going back, of course, and I guess most of us wouldn't want to if we could, even though we're acutely conscious of mistakes we've made. We have to remember that each of us is new at this business of living and content ourselves with the fact that most of us have plenty of time to make good decisions in the future.

If there's a rule in making decisions, I suppose it would be to listen to that inner voice and try to make decisions that tend to be growth-oriented. There's really no standing still, even if we'd like to.

I wonder how many mothers in poor families have said to their children, "I want you to get an education and make something of yourselves." The old term "make something of yourself" carries with it the clear message that we invent—that we make—ourselves.

I do think, however, that most try to play it safe, that is, select those decisions that seem to carry the least risk of failure; and by doing so, they live out their lives well below their real potential as persons. Sayings such as "I'm not going to stick my neck out" and "Don't rock the boat"—to say nothing of the popular "Take it easy" and "Never volunteer"—all indicate a reluctance to live fully extended or at the leading edge of life.

In business, every time a suggestion is made that involves any sort of innovation, some old-timer will ask,

"Who else is doing it?" He needs reassurance that the idea is not completely new, that it's been tested by someone else before he'll venture a "yes" vote.

Professor Sidney Hood writes, *"My observations lead me to the conclusion that human beings have suffered greater deprivations from their fear of life than from its abundance."*

A SELF-ACTUALIZED PERSON

What would it be like to be a fully mature, self-actualizing, fully functioning human being? This is the ideal, busy, happy person with all their faculties smoothly functioning in perfect cooperation—no wars going on inside, no hang-ups, no neuroses—the ideal, productive person.

Dr. Abraham Maslow made a study of self-actualized people, and they stack up this way:

First, these superior people have the ability to see life clearly, to see it as it is rather than as they wish it to be. They are less emotional and more objective about their observations. They are far above average in their ability to judge people correctly and to see through the phony or the fake. Usually, their choice of marriage partners is far better than average, although by no means perfect.

These self-actualized people are more accurate in their prediction of future events. They see more fully, and their judgment extends to an understanding of art, music, politics, and philosophy.

Self-actualized people see life clearly, judge well, are humble, creative and dedicated.

Yet they have a kind of humility—the ability to listen carefully to others, to admit they don't know everything and that others can teach them. This concept can be described as a childlike simplicity and lack of arrogance. Children have this ability to hear without preconception or earthly judgment. As the child looks out upon the world with wide, uncritical, innocent eyes, simply noting or observing that is the case, without either arguing the matter or demanding that it be otherwise, so do self-actualizing people look upon human nature in themselves and in others.

Without exception, Maslow found self-actualizing people to be dedicated to some work, task, duty, or vocation that they considered important. Because they were interested in this work, they worked hard, and yet the usual distinction between work and play became blurred. For them, work is exciting and pleasurable.

Maslow found creativity to be a universal characteristic of all the self-actualizing people he studied. Creativeness was almost synonymous with the terms healthy, self-actualizing, and fully human.

Here again, the creativity of these people is similar to that of little children before they have learned to fear the ridicule of others. Maslow believes this to be a characteristic that is too frequently lost as we grow older. Self-actualizing people either do not lose this fresh naïve approach; or if they lose it, they recover it later in life.

Spontaneity is typical of this person. Self-actualizing people are less inhibited and therefore more expressive, natural, and simple. And of course, they have courage. The courage that is needed in the lonely moments of creation. This is a kind of dating, a going out in front all alone, a defiance, a challenge. Thus, while these persons are humble in that they are open to new ideas, they are willing to forego popularity to stand up for a new idea.

The self-actualizing person has a low degree of self-conflict. This person is not at war with himself; his personality is integrated. This gives him more energy for productive purposes. As Maslow puts it, "Truth, goodness and beauty are in the average person in our culture only fairly well correlated with each other, and in the neurotic person even less so. It is only in the evolved and mature human being, in the self-actualizing, fully functioning person, that they are so highly correlated that for all practical purposes they may be said to fuse into a unity."

Research indicates that the healthy person is most integrated when facing a great creative challenge, some worthwhile goal, or a time of serious threat or emergency.

The psychologically healthy person is both selfish and unselfish, and in fact, these two attitudes merge into one. The healthy person finds happiness in helping others. Thus, for him, unselfishness is selfish. They get selfish pleasures from the pleasures of other people, which is a way of being unselfish. Or, saying it another way, the healthy person is selfish in a healthy way, a way that is beneficial to him and to society, too.

What are the qualities of a self-actualized person? This person possesses:

- The ability to see life clearly

- A childlike simplicity and lack of arrogance

- Dedication to some work that
  they consider important

- The creativity of children

- Spontaneity and courage

- A low degree of self-conflict

- Both selfishness and unselfishness

CLEAN THE SLATE

The mature person strives for strength—strength of purpose, strength of mind, and strength of character. Only these
can give us peace and serenity, joy and accomplishment.

I remember as a child in school watching my teacher
write the word "ain't" on the blackboard. Then she had all
of us look at the word for a long time. Finally, very slowly,
she erased it. As she did, she told us to erase it from our
minds, never to use it again. As the word disappeared from
the blackboard, it disappeared from our minds. I've never
forgotten the incident and how effective it was.

From time to time, we all need to clean the slate of our
lives—to face up to and then wipe away certain emotions

Face up to and then wipe away all detrimental emotions and habits holding you back.

and unrewarding habits of thinking and behavior that hold us back. Some of these things that need to be wiped away can sour and spoil our lives and rob us of the success we seek.

I read a story once about a man who decided to do something about an enormous piece of granite that rose up out of the ground near his house. He got a chisel and a hammer, and before long he had carved an excellent reproduction of an elephant. His neighbor and passersby were amazed because it looked for all the world like a real elephant grazing in his yard.

A friend asked the amateur sculptor how he ever managed to reproduce so faithfully the form of an elephant without a model to go by. The man replied, "I just chipped away everything that didn't look like an elephant."

To build a rich and rewarding life for ourselves, there are certain qualities and bits of knowledge that we need to acquire. But there are also things—harmful attitudes, superstitions, emotions—that we need to chip away. A person needs to chip away everything that doesn't look like the person he or she most wants to become.

STRIVE FOR STRENGTH

The mature person strives for strength—strength of purpose, strength of mind, and strength of character. Only these can give us peace and serenity, joy and accomplishment.

In cutting things away, an excellent place to begin is with animosity toward others. Getting rid of hatred and animosity is like putting down a hundred-pound weight. We may hurt no one else by hating, but we do serious damage to ourselves. It shows in the face, in the attitude, and in the person's life. Ulcers, high blood pressure, colitis, and heart disease are physical ailments that can often be traced to hate and even minor resentments. Beyond that, these harmful emotions can strangle a person's creative ability and will to win.

It is the unfailing mark of the little person—the person who has failed to grow—to spend his life dreaming and plotting about "getting even" for real or fancied injuries. History shows that a person who wants revenge brings it only upon himself.

Abraham Lincoln was famous for not holding a grudge. He put his political enemies, Stanton, Seward, and Chase, into his presidential cabinet.

Benjamin Disraeli, England's brilliant prime minister, did favors for many who bitterly opposed him. He said, "I never trouble to be avenged. When a man injures me, I put his name on a slip of paper and lock it up in a drawer. It is marvelous to see how the men I have so labeled have a knack of disappearing."

In cleaning the slate of our lives, we should do all in our power to get rid of hate, self-pity, guilt, and remorse. All that we have is the present moment and the future. They can be anything we want them to be.

Strength of purpose, mind, and character gives us peace and serenity, joy and accomplishment.

THE WONDERS OF PRAISE

We should try to find some way to commend those we love every day. Praise to a human being represents what sunlight, water, and soil are to a plant—the climate in which we grow best.

One day a few years back, I stopped my car for gas at a service station in Hollywood, California. While the middle-aged owner of the station cheerfully went about taking care of my car's needs, I noticed the station, although not new, was spotlessly clean. I was particularly surprised at the driveway—it was as clean as if my car was the first to use it.

I asked the owner how in the world he managed to keep the driveway spotless with dozens of cars dropping oil and tracking the dirt of the highways on it. He told me how a common product, sold in every supermarket, was in his estimation the best driveway cleaner in the world. He beamed in response to my comment on the way he kept his place of business. It was a valuable moment for both of us: I learned something of value, and he experienced the pleasure of honest praise.

The need for praise is basic to everyone. With it, a person blooms and grows. Without it, we tend to shrink and withdraw into ourselves.

We all know children need constant praise and encouragement. When a child brings home a piece of artwork that looks for all the world like an unfortunate accident, he still expects an encouraging word. But his need for encouragement is no less than his mother's or father's. Far too many parents are not getting any praise, or at least not nearly enough.

Understanding the importance of self-esteem and seeing the never-ending need for reaffirmation of a person's worth, we should make it our business to watch for honest opportunities to give praise—especially to the members of our families and those with whom we work.

There is a subtle but enormously valuable byproduct or backfire to this sort of thing: In order to praise others, we need to look for the good. It forces us to concentrate on what's right with people and the things they do rather than on what's wrong. It focuses our attention on the positive side of the ledger and, as a result, makes us happier, more productive, and more pleasant to be around. Then, too, people like those who praise them and recognize their value. When we give praise, we attract a larger circle of friends. And finally, giving praise is the best known way to receive it. It's hard for anyone to compliment a chronic grouch.

Whenever you hear someone say, "Nobody appreciates me; nobody gives me credit for all I do," the chances are he is so wrapped up in himself and in getting happiness from others, he has completely forgotten how to give.

Try to commend those you love every day. Praise is the climate in which we grow best. We do not just want it, we need it like we need the air we breathe.

Make it your business to watch for honest opportunities to give praise.

Molière said, "The most agreeable recompense which we can receive for things which we have done is to see them known, to have them applauded with praises which honor us."

DEVELOPING TWO GREAT FACTORS

If we would develop heart and mind, learn to love greatly and think clearly, everything else would be added to us— everything we want and more than we need.

There's a small paperback book, edited by Erich Fromm, titled *The Nature of Man*, in which appears the following statement: "People tend to achieve their human potential insofar as they develop love and reason." It might be a good time to ask ourselves how well we're doing in those departments. To the extent that we develop love and reason will we realize our potential as persons. These are the faculties that are uniquely human and on which you and I must depend if we're to achieve what we were designed to achieve.

We tend to think of developing human potential along lines more closely associated with kinds of work or sports, and perhaps that's part of it. But it's the development of heart and mind that can raise us to new levels of humanness. If we would develop heart and mind, learn to love greatly and think clearly, everything else would be added to us—everything we want and more than we need. Most

The development of heart and mind can raise you to new levels of fulfillment.

importantly, there would be peace and loving-kindness in all our relations with others.

If you think about it, you'll realize that those whose lives are marked by lack in the midst of abundance are those who have not discovered—who have not developed in themselves—the capacities for love and reason.

And if someone should ask you, "How does a person develop his or her potential?" you can reply, "By developing love and reason." With those two capacities alone, the fulfillment is there. We have only to think of the truly great people we have known personally: the great teacher; perhaps a relative, a friend, a parent, a fellow worker, or the stranger who appeared out of nowhere to help us out of a bad situation and who then quietly disappeared, leaving only the memory of a smile and that calm willingness to help.

When we think of the person who has developed love and reason to an uncommonly high degree in his or her life, we invariably think of someone who has a calm, even serene way of looking at things, studying things, before making a decision.

Such people give of themselves freely, unstintingly, and they reap an abundant harvest in return. They tend to be quiet people, although they can laugh and enjoy themselves as much as anyone—more, really, because they see more in their surroundings, notice more about the people with whom they associate. They are more understanding and more forgiving and look for the reasons behind events, rather than just at the events themselves.

People tend to achieve their human potential as they develop love and reason.

People tend to achieve their human potential insofar as they develop love and reason. People with closed minds, on any subject, are stuck somewhere along the way.

SELF AND/OR GROUP CONVERSATION STARTERS

1. Have you tried to "go home again"? Was it still a good fit? What was different? Will it ever be the same as you imagined? If you never left, why not?

2. Have you "made something of yourself"? Are you in the process of inventing and/or reinventing yourself? Do you have a "new you" in mind that will fulfill your goals for the future?

3. Write what you believe is a "fully mature, self-actualizing, fully functioning human being— the ideal, busy, happy, productive person." Do you see yourself becoming that person?

4. How many of the seven qualities of a self-actualized person do you possess? If not all seven, will you choose to work on developing those qualities in your life?

5. Are you committed to ridding yourself of hate, self-pity, guilt, and remorse? How imbedded are these negative qualities in your psyche? Deeply? Slightly?

6. Do you routinely praise others? How praiseworthy are you?

MENTAL HEALTH AND HAPPINESS

MENTALLY HEALTHY QUALITIES

A **study performed** by two doctors at the Menninger Foundation came up with a prescription for good mental health. According to this study, mentally healthy people behave consistently in five important ways.

Number one: They have a wide variety of sources of gratification.

This does not mean that they move frenetically from one activity to another but that they find pleasure in many different ways and from many different things. If for any reason they lose some of their sources of gratification, they have others to which they can turn.

Number two: Mentally healthy people are flexible under stress.

This simply means that they can roll with the punches. When faced with problems, they see alternate solutions. Flexibility under stress is closely related to having a wide variety of sources of gratification. With more supports on which to fall back, a person is less threatened by situations that produce fear and anxiety.

Number three: They recognize and accept their limitations and their assets.

Put another way, they have a reasonably accurate picture of themselves, and they like what they see. That does not mean that they're complacent or narcissistic but that they know they cannot be anyone else, and that's alright with them.

Number four: They treat other people as individuals.

People who are preoccupied with themselves pay only superficial attention to others. They're so tied up in themselves that they can't observe the subtleties of another person's feelings, nor can they really listen. Mentally healthy people really care about how other people are feeling.

People who are preoccupied with themselves pay only superficial attention to others.

Number five: Mentally healthy people are active and productive.

They use their resources on their behalf and on the behalf of others. They do what they do because they like to do it and enjoy using their skills. They do not feel driven to produce to prove themselves. They seek achievement for what they can do, not for what they can be. For when people try to be something or someone, they are never satisfied with themselves, even if they achieve their desired goal.

How many of these qualities do you have? If you're desiring to cultivate more of them, the best way to do so is to embrace life as a process of becoming. Live life to the fullest, pursuing self-actualization, simplicity, and truth, and you will likely enjoy good mental health.

NEUROSIS

A distinguished American psychotherapist has said that *"no one, as far as we know, is born neurotic. We've learned to become neurotic as a result of our upbringing. ... Our early self-concepts depend upon the concepts that others have toward us. If those who are important in the life of a child generally blame him, he will learn to blame himself. If they consistently accept him, he will learn to accept himself. That does not mean that the self-concept a child first learns is absolutely final.... He can later in life change*

Live life to the fullest, pursuing self-actualization, simplicity, and truth, and you will likely enjoy good mental health.

it...[but] this early self-concept...does tend to set the pattern for later attitudes and behavior."

I came across a great line the other day. It was written by Emanuel H. Demby, and it goes: *"Self-confidence is like a psychological credit card."* To tell youngsters that they are great is to give them the kind of self-image they need to build meaningful lives for themselves. Youngsters will discover their limitations, their blind spots, the areas in which they have little or no aptitude soon enough without our help. Neurosis is like a chain that we put on our children to hinder them in their development and activities.

If you'd like to examine yourself for traces of neurosis, Dr. Albert Ellis, in his book *How to Live with a "Neurotic" at Home and at Work*, gives a list of popular beliefs—irrational ideas, really—each of which indicates a neurosis. You can check your own beliefs against the list.

Remember, each of the following statements is *false* and suggests a neurosis:

- An adult must be approved of or loved by almost anyone for almost everything the person does. What others think of him or her is most important.

- Depending on others is better than depending on oneself.

- A person should be thoroughly competent, adequate, talented, and intelligent in all possible respects. Incompetence in

anything whatsoever is an indication that
a person is inadequate or worthless.

- The main goal and purpose in life
  is achievement/success.

- One should blame oneself severely for all
  mistakes and wrongdoings. Punishing oneself
  for errors will help prevent future mistakes.

- A person should blame others for their
  mistakes and bad behaviors and get upset
  about the errors and faults of others.

- Because a certain thing once strongly affected
  someone's life, it should affect it indefinitely.

- Because parents or society taught the
  acceptance of certain traditions, one must go
  on unthinkingly accepting these traditions.

- If things are not the way one would
  like them to be, it is a catastrophe.

- Other people should make things easier for us.

- No one should have to put off present
  pleasures for future gains.

- Avoiding life's difficulties and responsibilities
  is better than facing them.

- Inertia and inaction are necessary
  and/or pleasant.

- One should rebel against doing things, regardless of how necessary they are, if doing them is unpleasant.

- Happiness is usually externally caused or created by outside persons or events.

- A person has virtually no control over his or her emotions and cannot help feeling bad on many occasions.

- If something is or may be dangerous or injurious, one should be seriously concerned about it.

- Worrying about a possible danger will help ward it off or decrease its effect.

Well, how did you do?

Getting back to our saying that "self-confidence is a kind of psychological credit card," I don't think enough has been said about the power of positive expectation. It's truly amazing, and there's simply no explaining it, how when we confidently expect something worthwhile to materialize in our lives, it invariably does. It gives each of us a kind of magic wand with which we can bring all sorts of interesting and rewarding events and things into our lives. Those who have cultivated this power, who consciously and actively work at it regularly, do the most amazing things.

When we confidently expect something worthwhile to materialize in our lives, it invariably does.

"It takes courage to be happy."
-Mark Van Doren

We're often taught as youngsters to expect the worst. How many times have we heard someone say, "If you don't expect to succeed, you won't be disappointed"? If you have trouble confidently expecting a successful outcome, a reminder card placed where you'll see it every morning when you get up and at odd times throughout the day can help you get on course and form a very valuable new habit.

THE STRENGTH TO BE HAPPY

It is in the expectation of happiness that much of happiness itself is found. And it takes courage to expect happiness.

On the occasion of his 75th birthday, Mark Van Doren, the American writer, poet, critic, and educator, was interviewed by a reporter for *LIFE Magazine,* and one of the things he said stuck in my mind. I saved this.

He said, "It takes courage to be happy." Now in those six words he said a great deal. Any person can wallow in misery and self-pity. It's easy to rail against the world and its injustices. It's easier still to sit down and do nothing like the famous hound dog with its tail in the crack, but it takes courage to be happy.

When he said it takes courage to be happy, he didn't mean happiness today or tomorrow or a week from next Thursday. He meant to be happy as a general, relatively constant way of living; to be a happy person as opposed to a generally unhappy person.

And it does take courage—courage of a high order. The world is full, it seems, of the "it's too good to last" or "it's just my kind of luck" people who expect bad luck and rejection as confidently as they expect the sun to rise the next morning. They are people who were given bleak and disappointing starts in life.

Tolstoy said, "Man is meant for happiness and this happiness is in him, in the satisfaction of the daily needs of his existence." And La Rochefoucauld said, "Happiness is in the taste and not in the things themselves. We're happy from possessing what we like, not from possessing what others like."

In a passage that I think is very revealing, Jane Austin wrote, "No temper could be more cheerful than hers or possess in a greater degree that sanguine expectation of happiness, which is happiness itself." It is in the expectation of happiness that much of happiness itself is found. And it takes courage to expect happiness.

Balzac wrote, "All happiness depends on courage and work." I've had many periods of wretchedness, but with energy and, above all, with illusions, I've pulled through them all.

My old favorite, George Santayana said, "Happiness is the only sanction in life. Where happiness fails, existence remains a mad and lamentable experiment."

Bertrand Russell put it well when he said, "Contempt for happiness is usually contempt for other people's happiness and is an elegant disguise for hatred of the human race."

The Chinese philosopher, Lin Yutang, said, "I've always been impressed by the fact that the most studiously avoided subject in Western philosophy is that of happiness."

A French philosopher said much the same as did Mark Van Doren. He said, "To live, we must conquer incessantly. We must have the courage to be happy."

We've all seen people seriously handicapped in one way or another who are wonderfully cheerful and happy people. And we've wondered how they do it. We've said to ourselves, "I don't think I could be happy if I had his or her affliction." These people are happy because they are courageous and because they don't like the alternative.

NURTURE YOUR ABILITY TO LAUGH

I have found it a good rule of thumb to be slightly suspicious of anyone who takes himself too seriously. There's usually something fishy there someplace.

One of the enriching blessings of growing older all the time is that it has a way of improving one's sense of humor—or at least it should. The person without a good sense of humor is a person to avoid as though he were a known carrier of a plague.

Horace Walpole once said, "I have never yet seen or heard anything serious that was not ridiculous." And Samuel Butler said, "The one serious conviction that a man

Don't permit the dark side of things to dominate your life.

should have is that nothing is to be taken seriously." It has been said that "seriousness is the only refuge of the shallow." Oscar Wilde said, "It is a curious fact that the worst work is always done with the best intentions and that people are never so trivial as when they take themselves very seriously."

I remember that when I was in the service, one of the toughest jobs I had was to keep from laughing at the wrong times—during an admiral's inspection, for example. There is nothing funnier than the seriousness of the military, especially high-ranking military. The fancy costumes, the panoply, the shining sabers, the serious faces—it was all, to me, hilariously funny.

We can be serious about situations. When a youngster is ill or hurt or someone insults your spouse, you can get very serious about the situation in a hurry. But that's not taking ourselves seriously. That's different.

The thing that bothered me about Hemingway, as much as I admired his work, was that I thought he tended to take himself too seriously. He didn't seem to be able to laugh at himself. And I think he suffered from this flaw in his character.

I have found it a good rule of thumb to be slightly suspicious of anyone who takes himself too seriously. There's usually something fishy there someplace. I think this is why we love children so much—life is a game to them. They will do their best at whatever work is given to them, but they never seem to lose their ebullient sense of humor; there is always a sparkle of humor in their eyes. When a child lacks this, he is usually in need of help.

Dictators are famous for their lack of humor. The mark of a cruel person is that he doesn't seem to be able to see anything funny in the world. And a sense of humor was what was so great about Mark Twain. No matter how serious the subject, he could find the humor in it and bring it out. So could Will Rogers. All the great comedians have this ability to see what's funny in the so-called serious situation. They can poke fun at themselves. There are those who believe that a sense of humor is the only thing that has kept the human race from totally extinguishing itself.

People who are emotionally healthy with a sense of proportion are cheerful people. They tend to look upon the bright side of things and see a lot of humor in their daily lives. They're not Pollyannas; they know what's going on and that a lot of it's not at all funny, but they don't permit the dark side of things to dominate their lives. To my mind, when a person lacks a sense of humor, there's something pretty seriously wrong with him.

Samuel Butler said, "A sense of humor keen enough to show a man his own absurdities as well as those of other people will keep a man from the commission of all sins, or nearly all, save those that are worth committing." It took a sense of humor to write that, and only people with blank spaces where their senses of humor should be will find it offensive. There's something so healthy about laughter, especially when it's directed at ourselves. This form of humor was what made Jack Benny and Bob Hope such durable and successful comedians, along with many others going clear back to Charlie Chaplin.

I remember the wonderful ending to that really fine motion picture, *The Treasure of Sierra Madre*. After months of back-breaking toil and the constant danger of death from bandits, the characters find they have lost all the gold and that they're right back where they started from. And suddenly they begin to laugh. They almost faint from laughter. And you realize they've seen themselves in their true perspective—the ludicrousness of the situation and their former greed. And just as suddenly, you realize that everything is all right again as they part and go their separate ways.

There are times of seriousness for all of us when all the laughter seems to be gone, but we should not permit these periods to last too long. When we've lost our sense of humor, there isn't very much left. We become ridiculous. We must then go to war against the whole world, and that's a war we've got to lose.

SELF AND/OR GROUP
CONVERSATION STARTERS

1. Of the five mentally healthy qualities listed, how many do you fully equate with the level of your mental health? If changes are necessary, what steps will you take—immediately, within the week, the month—to improve your state of mind?

2. Confidently expecting something worthwhile will usually materialize. Has this been proven true in your life? Has the opposite also been true when you expect the negative?

3. Of all the quotes in this chapter about happiness, which one or two will you write in a journal, your calendar, or somewhere to keep it close as a reminder?

4. Are you happy in general, leading a relatively happy lifestyle? What distinguishes that type of outlook on life, according to some of the quotations in the chapter?

5. On a scale from 1 (poor) to 10 (great), how would you rank your sense of humor? How would your best friend rank your sense of humor?

6. "When we've lost our sense of humor, there isn't very much left. We become ridiculous. We must then go to war against the whole world, and that's a war we've got to lose." What do you think the author is saying in these few sentences? Write in your own words.

UNEARTH YOUR POTENTIAL

'd like to quote something to you from George B. Leonard's excellent book *Education and Ecstasy.* He asks, "Who is this creature we would educate so joyfully? What are his capacities? Can he really be changed? Will great efforts yield great gains? History tells us more than we want to know about what is wrong with man, and we can hardly turn a page in the daily press without learning the specific time, place, and name of evil. But perhaps the most pervasive evil of all rarely appears in the news. This evil, the waste of human potential, is particularly painful to recognize, for it strikes our parents and children, our friend and brothers, ourselves."

James Agee wrote: "I believe that every human being is potentially capable, within his 'limits,' of fully 'realizing' his potentialities; that this, his being cheated and choked of it, is infinitely the ghastliest, commonest, and most inclusive of all the crimes of which the human world can accuse itself. I know only that murder is being done against nearly every individual on the planet."

To doubt is less painful than to rage. Throughout much of history, the safe, the authoritative, the official viewpoint has pronounced man limited, flawed, and essentially unchangeable. Each age has found ways of comforting men with pessimism. Accept limits, the wise men say, to keep from over-reaching yourselves or going mad with hope.

But hope and the awareness of wasted potential have never really faded from consciousness. Ever since the race of man first learned to wonder, men have been haunted by this irrepressible dream: that the limits of human ability lie beyond the boundaries of the imagination; that every human being uses only a tiny fraction of his abilities; that there must be some way for everyone to achieve far more of what is truly his to achieve.

History's greatest prophets, mystics, and saints have dreamed even more boldly, saying that all men are some-how one with God. The dream has survived history's failures, ironies, and uneven triumphs, sustained more by intuition than by what our scientific-rationalist society calls "facts."

Now, however, the facts are beginning to come in. Science has at last turned its attention to the central questions of human capability, has begun the search for a technology as well as a science of the human potential. Men in varied fields, sometimes unknown to each other, sometimes disagreeing on method, philosophy, and even language, are coming to startlingly similar conclusions that make pessimism about the human prospect far more difficult than before.

These men—neurologists, psychologists, educators, philosophers, and others—are making what may well be the century's biggest news. Almost all of them agree that people now are using less than 10 percent of their potential abilities. Some put the figure at less than 1 percent. The fact of the matter is that anyone who makes a responsible and systematic study of the human animal eventually feels the awe that moved Shakespeare to write, "What a piece of work is a man! How noble in reason! How infinite in faculty!"

THE NUMBER 1 QUALITY FOR SUCCESS

In talking about potential and ideas we may want to pass along to our kids, in school and more importantly in the home, of all of the qualities that parents can instill in children, which would you say is the most important?

Some time back, the editors of a business magazine concluded a survey on what qualities it takes to be successful, but since the survey was by the editors of a business magazine, it was naturally assumed that what was meant is success in business.

Well, interestingly enough, the same number 1 quality emerged for success in business that came up for success as a father or mother. And do you know what that single quality is? One word: *integrity.*

There are millions today who will laugh at that, but the odds are good that neither they nor their youngsters are doing too well.

Children who are taught the importance of integrity never seem to lose it. It becomes part of their being, their way of doing things, and more than anything else, it guarantees their success in life as persons.

Integrity is what a man wants in his wife and she in him. That's what we look for and hope for in a doctor or dentist, the person who designs and builds our home, the person we work for, and the people who work under us. It's what we want more than anything else in a politician or an appointed official, in judges and police officers.

Integrity is honesty—but much more than the superficial kind of honesty that keeps a person from stealing or cheating. Integrity is a state of mind and character that goes all the way through like good solid construction.

And integrity, or the lack of it, is generally taught in the home, in little as well as in big things. In business or in life, the No. 1 quality is integrity.

For most people, it would seem getting through life is a matter of managing a compromise between integrity and expediency. Integrity is all well and good, and everybody would like to have the word apply to her, but there

Integrity is a state of mind and character that goes all the way through like good solid construction.

are times when people think it's perhaps best to wink at integrity and indulge in a little larceny or remain silent—times when speaking one's mind might result in a loss of popularity or ostracism of some kind.

As José Ortega y Gasset tells it, "The human creature is born into the world in a natural state of disorientation. He's the only creature on earth who is not at home in his environment. He must and he does, in a godlike fashion, create his own life, his own world."

Now that's an awesome thing to think about. The responsibility is onerous, frightening. To prevent a white knight-like façade of unblemished and unsoiled integrity is not only difficult; to most people, I'm sure, it's also a little ridiculous. The old battle cry of the mob is, "Everybody does it. Why shouldn't I?" And that's exactly why the person of integrity doesn't do it. The crowd will ask, "What are you trying to be—a boy scout?" What's wrong with being a boy scout? Why shouldn't we go straight in a time when such an attitude needs all the recruits it can get?

Integrity in business is the surest way on earth to succeed. Sometimes it might seem that what you're doing is going to cut into profits, but it inevitably ends up increasing profits.

When we put the well-being of people in first place, we'll never make a mistake. People first, profit last. And the more you do it, the bigger and better your profits become. It's the old law of cause and effect. In my opinion, there should be courses on integrity.

Someone once wrote that if honesty didn't exist, it ought to be invented as the best means of getting rich.

But kids don't learn integrity when they see their father bringing home loot from his place of employment, or bragging about how he cheated on his income tax, or lifting towels and other loose impediments from a hotel or motel room.

In a product, a service, or a human being, integrity is priceless and can only lead to success in the long run. We've all played golf with people who conveniently forget strokes. They fool no one, least of all the other club members, and they become objects of derision.

And every week we read in the newspapers of men, quite often in high places, whose lack of basic integrity has landed them in trouble with the law, with resulting damage to themselves and the members of their family. They were not taught the importance of integrity as youngsters and failed to mature and learn the importance of it as adults.

DECIDOPHOBIA

One dilemma faced by most human beings in our modern society is the matter of making decisions. We've learned that ours is the only species on earth whose natural state is one of disorientation, and, therefore, all of us must create our own world, even if it consists of nothing more than playing copycat—closing our eyes and ears and blindly following the person in front of us, hoping that somehow he or the person he's following knows where he's going and that when they get there they'll both like it.

We'd like to think that we're intelligent and effective decision-makers. But the facts seem to indicate that we're not and that we use all kinds of dodges to keep from making decisions. According to Princeton philosopher Walter Kaufmann, who wrote a book entitled *Without Guilt and Justice: From Decidophobia to Autonomy*, there are ten major copouts that most of us use to avoid making decisions, and these ten avoidance techniques fall under the larger categories of Type A and Type B drifting. Type A drifters go through the motions every day without giving their routines any additional thought, whereas Type B drifters, also called "foolers," try to give the impression that they're in revolt against the so-called status quo by dropping out of life.

What we're seeking, as Professor Kaufmann points out, is autonomy—authenticity as sovereign persons. How does one go about making decisions on his own, decisions calculated to bring him face to face with the best possible life for him? He goes by his gut feelings. He listens to the voice within, knowing that Thoreau was right when he said, *"If one advances confidently in the direction of his dreams, and endeavors to live the life which he has imagined, he will meet with a success unexpected in common hours."* This means not sitting and wallowing in our old beliefs but moving out of them into new, fresh territory. It

Ask yourself: "Am I living by my standards or by the standards of those about me?"

means asking the question "Am I living by my standards or by the standards of those about me?"

Achievement is not the most important thing. Authenticity is. The authentic person experiences the reality of himself by knowing himself, being himself, and becoming a credible, responsive person. He actualizes his own unprecedented uniqueness and appreciates the uniqueness of others. This is what makes someone a winner.

While everyone has moments of autonomy, if only fleeting, winners are able to sustain their autonomy over ever-increasing periods of time. They may make the wrong decisions sometimes and lose ground occasionally, but in spite of these setbacks they maintain a basic faith in themselves and continue to make decisions accordingly.

Winners are not afraid to do their own thinking and to use their own knowledge. They can separate facts from opinion and don't pretend to have all the answers. They listen to others, evaluating what they say, but they come to their own conclusions. And while they can admire and respect other people, they are not totally defined, demolished, bound, or awed by them. Winners do not act helpless or play the blame game. Instead, they assume responsibility for their own life. They do not give others false authority over them. They are their own boss, and they know it.

They key word in our thinking, in our conduct, in our goals, and in our lives should be authenticity. We need to become what we are.

Winners do not act helpless or play the blame game. Instead, they assume responsibility for their own life.

HOW TO ACT LIKE A PRO

My old friend, Herb True, dropped into my office with some exciting thoughts. There are some people you just can't sit down with without getting all fired up—people who are interested in ideas and people.

He said that the pro, in whatever field he happens to work, doesn't follow standards; he sets them! And the first step toward becoming a pro in anything you want very much to do is to learn the rules.

He went on to say that the amateur is the person who doesn't know the rules, and what's even worse, he doesn't know that he doesn't know the rules.

The amateur, when he fails at what he does, says, "Well, that's the way the cookie crumbles." He finds ways of finding exterior reasons for his failures. We tend to look inside of ourselves to explain our successes and outside of ourselves to explain our failures. But the pro accepts responsibility for his actions.

There's the story of the football coach whose team had won four games in a row. When asked by reporters for his secret, the coach went into detail as to his superior methods of coaching, choosing men, and scouting. The following week, his team lost. When asked why, he said, "It rained." And one reporter asked, "Just on your team?"

The real pro would have said, "They fielded a better team than we did today." But the amateur is always scrambling for excuses. He spends his time looking outside of himself for reasons for his failures that could easily be used to bring about success the next time if he decided to turn pro and learn the rules.

The next mark of the real pro is that he has a definite code of conduct. This code is all set up and working. Whenever he comes upon a situation that violates his code, he passes it up. But he doesn't have to sit around and think about it, or try to rationalize it, or find excuses for doing something he knows very well he should not do. He's got a code of conduct, and he sticks by it.

For example, let's say he's in politics or on the police force. His code is that he will not accept bribes of any kind. If someone offers him a bribe, he instantly refuses it because it is a bribe. The amount of the bribe then becomes totally unimportant. Whether it's five dollars or five million dollars makes not the slightest difference.

Another mark of the pro is that he tries always to distinguish between the urgent and the important. Something may be, or may appear to be, very urgent, but is it really important? Is it important in a permanent, meaningful way? Or is its seeming urgency little more than a needless time consumer? Every act we perform during the day is either goal-achieving, tension-relieving, or unnecessary. The pro keeps an intelligent balance. He does this by making sure that the time he's supposed to be working, he's working. He enjoys his work, and he enjoys his leisure.

Yes, the real pro, in whatever he has chosen to do, does not follow the standards set by others. He sets his own. He knows that the precedents he sets will be broken some-day, just as he breaks those that have been established before.

Do you possess the characteristics of the "pro"? Do you:

- accept responsibility for your actions?

- have a definite code of conduct?

- distinguish between the urgent
  and the important?

When was the last time you set standards for your behavior?

SELF AND/OR GROUP
CONVERSATION STARTERS

1. Do you believe that you must accept limits to keep from "over-reaching yourself or going mad with hope"? Or do you believe that every person uses only a tiny fraction of their abilities and you can truly achieve much more than you can imagine?

2. Where does integrity fit in with your career, relationships, business dealings, communications, and such? Does your integrity tend to be "relative," in that it depends on the situation and/or the people involved?

3. Are you an intelligent and effective decision maker? Why or why not?

4. Do you make wise decisions quickly, after some consideration, after much consideration? If you make a wrong decision, are you likely to own up to it immediately? Shift the blame? Cover it up completely?

5. Are you a "real pro" as defined in the last section of the chapter? Define yourself as you see yourself as a pro. Do you possess the three characteristics of a pro?

6. Unearthing your potential in this
chapter revealed that:

- everyone has undiscovered or unused potential

- integrity in all areas of your life is vital

- decision making is an important
part of unlocking potential

- you must accept responsibility for your actions

- follow a code of conduct

7. Which one of these is the hardest to do/
believe? Which one is the easiest?

THE SHORT AND THE LONG OF MEMORY

A SHORT MEMORY IS GOOD AND BAD

Everything in nature has two sides—a good and a bad, a positive and a negative. In philosophy, this message goes back thousands of years to the Chinese yin and yang. The yang is the good—the sunny side of the hill; and the yin is the dark side. There is a dualism in everything in the universe. The rain that waters and fertilizes the crops also brings floods; the fire that warms our homes and cooks our meals causes widespread havoc when it's out of control.

And have you ever thought about the good and the bad sides of memory?

Each of us really has a very short memory. Sure, the subconscious remembers everything, but our conscious

There are two side to everything in nature— including memory.

minds forget. We forget the bad, and that's good. We forget our failures, our mistakes, our foolishness, the pain we've caused, the opportunities we've missed, the love we've failed to give when it was needed. These things pass from our conscious memory as though from a filter to which they cling for a while and then are cleansed away by time.

But we also forget, to our pain, the good, and that's bad. We forget the principles, the systems which, if we will but live by them daily, will result in our achieving the things we want to achieve. We literally forget how to live successfully.

If, through some diabolical device, we were constantly reminded of all of our past failures and mistakes, we would live in a state of constant depression, fear, and sorrow—a hell on earth. But instead, our conveniently forgetful minds save us from this.

But if, through some wonderful agency, we could be constantly reminded only of the good, of those principles and systems that we know work to our benefit and the benefit of society, we would live in a state of optimism, enthusiasm, and hope. We would go from one success to another.

Well, it's a fact that the world's most successful people manage to accomplish this latter state. They manage to arrange their minds so that they constantly remind themselves of what they're doing and where they're going. They know for certain that if they'll just do certain things in a certain way every day, they will be led to the goals toward which they're striving.

Successful people know that doing things in a certain way every day will lead to achieving their goals.

Most news seems to be bad. Our news headlines are not filled with all the good that's going on in the world. That would be kind of silly, I suppose. They report all the news, and the great majority of it seems to be on the negative side: wars, murders, crime, disasters, accidents, swindles, scandals.

Additionally, most people are so constituted, or so lacking in the proper education, that they, too, seem to act and talk rather on the negative side, and we're influenced by them. If we live then in accordance with our environment, we'll tend to forget the good and dwell on the bad the majority of the time. This means we will live most of our lives on the dark side of the ancient Chinese hill.

What's the solution?

It is to find a way to remind ourselves every day, as do the really successful, of those things that lead to success, to the good. Otherwise, we'll forget the good along with the bad.

THE TWELVE THINGS TO REMEMBER

The following are twelve things to remember, by Marhsall Field, entrepreneur and founder of very successful department store chain:

1. The value of time.

2. The success of perseverance.

3. The pleasure of working.

4. The dignity of simplicity.

5. The worth of character.

6. The power of kindness.

7. The influence of example.

8. The obligations of duty.

9. The wisdom of economy.

10. The virtue of patience.

11. The improvement of talent.

12. The joy of originating.

Good list, isn't it? It could be the kind of checklist that a person might carry and glance at from time to time. None of us is smart enough to remember all we know, as Will Rogers once said, "We all need reminding."

The value of time. At first you might think that applies to working, which it does for part of the time, but it also applies to time spent not working—time spent thinking, or dreaming, or relaxing, or reading, or walking, or indulging in a favorite hobby. The value of time...not to waste it on things that do nothing to help or bring enjoyment.

The success of perseverance. Perseverance can accomplish anything. My friend W. Clement Stone tells the story of Tom, who was born without half of a right foot and only a stub of a right arm. As a boy, he wanted to engage in sports as the other boys did. He had a burning desire to play football, of all things. Because of this desire, his parents had an artificial foot made for him. It was made of wood. The wooden foot was encased in a special stubby football shoe. Hour after hour, day after day, he would practice kicking the football with his wooden foot. He would try, and keep on trying, to make field goals from greater and greater distances. He became so proficient that he was hired by the New Orleans Saints.

Now, just offhand, what would you say a person's chances of playing professional football were if he were born without half of a right foot and a withered arm? But the screams of 66,910 football fans would be heard throughout the entire United States when Tom Dempsey, with his crippled leg, kicked the longest field goal ever kicked in a professional football game, within the last two seconds of the game, to give the Saints a winning score of nineteen to seventeen over the Detroit Lions. "We were beaten by a miracle," said Detroit coach Joseph Schmidt. But they were beaten by perseverance.

The pleasure of working. Often the pleasure that comes from working only comes after the work has been finished, but it's a pleasure you can't find any other way.

The dignity of simplicity. If only more people could learn to keep things simple, straightforward, honest. It's best in everything from architecture to living.

The worth of character goes without saying. It is the one thing each of us can build for himself that gives value to his life and himself.

The power of kindness to touch others.

The influence of example. The example set by parents will have a much greater influence on the life of a child than all the schooling in the world. The secret is, don't tell him; show him.

The obligations of duty gives meaning to our lives.

The wisdom of economy. This ties in with the dignity of simplicity.

The virtue of patience. Half the problems of the world could be prevented by patience. Give it a little time, and it will usually come out fine.

The improvement of talent. That's how we grow and mature at whatever we have chosen of our own free will to do with our lives.

And *the joy of originating.*

Great list—twelve things to remember that will definitely improve your outlook and results in life.

Half the problems of the world could be prevented by patience. Give it a little time, and it will usually come out fine.

SELF AND/OR GROUP CONVERSATION STARTERS

1. After reading about the good and the bad sides of memory, how many other examples can you think of?

2. What are your two worst memories? What are your two best memories? Which two come to mind the most? Least?

3. Have you managed to arrange your mind so that you constantly remind yourself of what you're doing and where you're going— like most successful people have done?

4. People today are bombarded with "news" 24/7, the great majority of which is negative. How does this affect your outlook? What would be better stimuli for your memory bank to absorb going forward?

5. Of the twelve things to remember, which one has made, or could make, the most positive difference in your life right now?

6. Of the twelve things to remember, which one hasn't made, or won't make, any difference in your life?

WHO WANTS TO LIVE WITH A HORSE?

The words **"know thyself"** are still two of the most important words ever put together. Do you know why people sometimes—quite often, as a matter of fact—have inferiority complexes? It's because their thinking is based on a false premise. The false premise is that they compare themselves to other people, when this is actually something they should never do, since no two human beings are alike. Everybody on earth is inferior to everyone else on earth in certain areas and superior in other areas.

A wise man once wrote, "To be human is to feel inferior." This is why the well-adjusted person, the person who knows himself, isn't bothered because he can't dance as well as so-and-so, or play golf or bridge as well as someone

It is completely impossible for any one human being to be as good at everything as all other human beings.

else. It would be completely impossible for any one human being to be as good at everything as every other human being.

The well-adjusted person admires others for their talents and abilities without feeling envious. In fact, he doesn't bring himself into comparison at all. He is happily resigned to the fact that he is not the best-looking, best-built, smartest, most talented, fastest, cleverest, funniest, most engaging person on earth.

Without even thinking about it, the well-adjusted person seems to know that every person is a potpourri of strengths and weaknesses inherited from all his ancestors. No two of them were alike, but each one had a slightly different strong point with the standard collection of weaknesses.

In his fine book *Psycho-Cybernetics*, Dr. Maxwell Maltz wrote:

> "Inferiority and superiority are reverse sides of the same coin. The cure lies in realizing that the coin itself is spurious...you are not 'inferior' [or] are not 'superior.' You are simply you.
>
> "You as a personality are not in competition with any other personality simply because there is not another person on the face of the earth like you or in your particular class. You are an individual. You are unique. You are not 'like' any other person. You are not 'supposed' to be

like any other person, and no other person is 'supposed' to be like you."

The doctor went on to write,

"God did not create a standard person and in some way label that person by saying, 'This is it.' He made every human being individual and unique, just as He made every snowflake individual and unique.

"God created short people and fat people, black, yellow, red, and white people. He has never indicated any preference for any one size, shape or color. Abraham Lincoln once said, 'God must have loved the common people, for He made so many of them.' He was wrong. There is no 'common man'—no standardized, common pattern. He would have been nearer the truth had he said, 'God must have loved uncommon people, for He made so many of them.'"

Anybody could make themselves feel inferior if they didn't realize that they are unlike any other human being who ever lived on earth. If they understand—fully and completely, intellectually and emotionally—that they each are a unique and different individual, no one can have an inferiority complex. How could they, since there's no standard against which to judge if every person is different? And every person *is* different.

An inferiority complex is a phantom—a ghost with no real substance.

Nothing on earth happens purely by accident. A person is living because he was meant to live, and he has talents and abilities that are his own—unique with him. His job, then, as a person is to learn to know himself. If he does, he will like himself, for he will discover he's quite a person after all. He will recognize and accept the things he cannot do as well as some other people, but he will also understand and appreciate those things it has been given him to do well. He will accept himself for what he really is—one of a kind, as different from every other person on earth as his fingerprints or his signature.

A human being is the finest, the noblest, the most godlike creature ever produced on earth. Not to be thankful for such a gift is the worst kind of ignorance. And an inferiority complex is a phantom—a ghost with no real substance. In the light of knowledge, it disappears.

THE FUTILITY OF CRITICISM

When we criticize another person, we set ourselves above that person; we become the figure of authority and place the other person in an inferior position. The best rule to use when criticism springs to your mind is to wait.

I've got some advice here for you today on how to become hated—how to stir up resentments and ill will that will simmer and hang on for years. All you have to do is...criticize!

Criticism puts people on the defensive, wounds their pride, and arouses resentment.

No matter what a person has done, or how they live their life, no one wants—or needs—criticism. This is why a criminal can fly into a rage against witnesses, prosecuting attorneys, and judges. Although he may have committed the most serious crime and knows full well that he has committed it, he deeply resents those who by their actions are critical of him.

The unfaithful husband or wife will, as often as not, fly into a wounded, self-pitying snit when confronted with evidence of his or her infidelity.

I'm not saying that people should not be criticized for criminal or moral misconduct. But I am saying that criticism makes a person try to justify himself, wounds his precious pride, hurts his sense of importance, and thoroughly arouses his resentment against the person or persons doing the criticizing.

When we criticize another person, we set ourselves above them and automatically put the other person on the defensive. And even if the person doesn't say anything and accepts the criticism meekly, it rankles.

When the husband at the bridge table says to his wife, "Well, my dear, you bid that hand like a certified moron," she might not say anything. She might not say anything at the moment, that is, but she's secretly praying for a miracle that will deliver a sawed-off shotgun into her hands. The other players squirm in embarrassment. And what does it accomplish? As Junius wrote, "It behooves the minor critic who hunts for blemishes to be a little distrustful of his own sagacity."

To withhold criticism is the way to greatness and earn the respect and/or love of others.

The best rule to use when criticism springs to your mind is to wait. Wait a while and try to look for the reasons behind the act you would criticize. It's also a good time to ask oneself, "Who am I to be criticizing others? Am I really all that great and pure and all-knowing and perfect?" By all means wait until the heat of anger has dissipated. This is one of the world's most difficult things to do, and it takes a very mature person to master the wisdom and self-control to withhold criticism. But it's the way to greatness and one of the best known ways to earn the respect and/or love of others.

People know when they've done something wrong or foolish, and they usually know that you know it, too. And when you refrain from being critical, they're grateful; they respect you. As often as not, they'll be much tougher on themselves and make a concerted effort to avoid making the same mistake again. It's been said that the legitimate aim of criticism is to direct attention to the excellent. The bad will dig its own grave, and the imperfect may safely be left to that final neglect from which no amount of present undeserved popularity can rescue it.

As Epictetus put it, "Do not give sentence in another tribunal till you have been yourself judged in the tribunal of Justice." The key to overcoming the urge to criticize others is to wait. Wait a minute, or an hour, or a day...or forever.

WHY YOU DON'T HAVE TO BE A LONER

My father was a regular and an avid reader of the old Zane Grey books (that's how I got hold of them), which invariably, or so it seemed, began with a stranger riding into town. He was tall, lean, and always covered with alkali dust. Cool gray eyes peered evenly from under straight brows, and his hand hovered near the six-gun strapped to his thigh.

He had no friends or acquaintances and seemed to like it that way. He was a man of few words and kept his own counsel. His world consisted of little more than himself and his horse and the bad guy he was usually after.

It makes a good story, and everyone seems to be intrigued by this sort of man of mystery. But, in real life, it's a lonely way to live, especially since few of us have horses these days.

You cannot know too many people. And we'd all be better off if we could overcome our natural timidity where strangers are concerned, if we could open up more.

As a friend of mine who has attained an unusually high position in the world says, "Open the doors and windows of your mind and heart to others, and you'll reap a wonderful harvest of friends."

Many of us have a tendency to speak or smile only after another person has spoken or smiled at us first. We tend to be reactive instead of proactive. It reminds me of the person who sat in front of the cold stove and said, "Give me heat, and then I'll add the wood."

"Open the doors and windows of your mind and heart to others, and you'll reap a wonderful harvest of friends."

The world just doesn't work that way. With a little effort, a person can form the habit of smiling and saying "hello" first. Nineteen times out of twenty, you'll get a favorable response.

I know a man who was the foreign representative for an American electronics firm. He was something of an introvert, and on his frequent flights all over the world, he'd bury himself in a book to keep from having to talk to the passenger next to him.

On one trip, a friendly Englishman managed to get a conversation started with him. It turned out that the Englishman was on an electronics buying trip to the States, and a large order resulted. Then and there he decided to change his attitude toward strangers. While it may not result in another business deal, he's meeting all sorts of interesting people and making many new friends.

We should never say, "He's not my kind of person" or "That's not my sort of crowd." Wherever there's a human being, there's a human story, and it's invariably interesting and informative. It stretches our minds, broadens our horizons, and adds to our collection of acquaintances and friends.

And all it takes is a smile, the word "hello," and a comment or two to get a conversation going. The chances are that the other person is as anxious to add to his collection of friends as we are. But he or she may be just a little on the timid side, as many people are in the presence of strangers. It's true: you can't know too many people. As we grow older, we should cultivate all the friends we can.

You can't know too many people; we should cultivate all the friends we can.

The person who shuts others out of their life ends up shutting themselves in. Try my friend's advice. Throw open the doors and windows of your mind and heart to others, and reap a harvest of friends.

Who wants to live with a horse?

SELF AND/OR GROUP CONVERSATION STARTERS

1. How well do you know yourself? Are you happily resigned to the fact that you're not the best-looking, best-built, smartest, most talented, fastest, cleverest, funniest, most engaging person on earth?

2. Do you accept yourself for who you really are—one of a kind, as different from every other person on earth as your fingerprints, signature, and DNA?

3. Are you prone to criticize others? Yourself? What are the usual results of your criticism?

4. It takes a very mature person to master the wisdom and self-control to withhold criticism. How mature are you regarding this issue? Very mature? Somewhat mature? Totally immature?

5. Do you consider yourself a loner? Do you think you need to be friendlier? Are you more comfortable at home alone or in the company of friends and/or family? Explain each of your answers.

6. Are you usually the first one to smile and say hello to a stranger? If not, explain why you hold back.

WOE BE GONE

Two young boys were raised by an alcoholic father. As they grew older, they moved away from that broken home, each going his own way in the world. Several years later, they happened to be interviewed separately by a psychologist who was analyzing the effects of drunkenness on children in broken homes.

His research revealed that the two men were strikingly different from each other. One was a clean-living teetotaler, the other a hopeless drunk like his father. The psychologist asked each of them why he developed the way he did, and each gave an identical answer: "What else would you expect when you have a father like mine?"

That story was revealed by Dr. Hans Selye, internationally renowned Canadian physician and scientist known as the "father of stress." A medical pioneer, he devoted the majority of his years to the exploration of biological stress. And he

"...how you react to each circumstance you encounter that determines the result."

related the story of the two sons of the drunken father in an article for *New Realities*. And the story demonstrates a cardinal rule implicit in stress, health, and human behavior.

According to R. H. Schuller, "It is not what happens to you in life that makes the difference. It is how you react to each circumstance you encounter that determines the result. Every human being in the same situation has the possibilities of choosing how he will react—either positively or negatively."

Thus, stress is not necessarily caused by stressor agents; rather, it is caused by the way stressor agents are perceived, interpreted, or appraised in each individual case. Outside events and people upset some more than others, because they are looked upon and dealt with in entirely different ways. The stressors may even be the same in each case, yet the reaction will almost always be different in different people.

So what is the cause of our stress? The outside agents and people or the perception and interpretation each person brings to a given situation? If a microbe is in or around us all the time and yet causes no disease until we are exposed to stress, what is the cause of our illness—the microbe or the stress?

Basowitz, Persky, Korchin, and Grinker, in their book *Anxiety and Stress,* have this to say about the cause of stress:

> The stress accruing from a situation is based...
> on the way the affected subject perceives it;

perception depends upon the multiplicity of factors, including the genetic equipment, basic individual needs and longings, earlier conditioning influences and a host of life experiences and cultural pressures. No one of these can be singled out for exclusive emphasis. The common denominator of "stress disorders" is reaction to circumstances of threatening significance to the organism."

Armed with that information, it would seem that we can greatly improve our reactions to stressful situations. What seems to be a cruel world to one person might be filled with challenge and opportunity to another. It is our reaction that makes the difference.

ONLY 8 PERCENT OF WORRIES ARE WORTH IT

According to the Bureau of Standards, "A dense fog covering seven city blocks, to a depth of 100 feet, is composed of something less than one glass of water." That is, all the fog covering seven city blocks, at 100 feet deep, could be, if it were gotten all together, held in a single drinking glass. It would not quite fill it. And this could be compared to our worries. If we can see into the future and if we could see our problems in their true light, they wouldn't tend to

Most worries are not really worth too much; we can manage to solve the important ones.

blind us to the world, to living itself, but instead could be relegated to their true size and place. And if all the things most people worry about were reduced to their true size, you could probably put them all into a water glass, too.

It's a well-established fact that as we get older, we worry less. We learn, with the passing of the years and the problems each of them yields, that most of our worries are not really worth bothering ourselves about too much and that we can manage to solve the important ones.

But to younger people, they often find their lives obscured by the fog of worry. Yet here's an authoritative estimate of what most people worry about:

- things that never happen, 40 percent—
  that is, 40 percent of the things you
  worry about will never occur anyway;

- things over and past that can't be changed
  by all the worry in the world, 30 percent;

- needless worries about our health, 12 percent;

- petty, miscellaneous worries, 10 percent;

- real, legitimate worries, 8 percent.

Only 8 percent of your worries are worth concerning yourself about. Ninety-two percent are pure fog with no substance at all.

The wife or husband will nurse and cling to things that have happened or have been said in the past and keep exhuming them like desiccated corpses. If the collection gets large enough—and it could easily get large enough in even the best of households—if a person never forgets every little slight or oversight or word spoken in impatience or anger, the marriage will wind up on the rocks.

The largest cause of all arguments in the home, incidentally, is worry about money. And this wouldn't be such a problem—in fact, it could be a source of gratification—if we could just learn to live within our means and save a part of every dollar we earn. It isn't easy, but it will get rid of the worries and most of the argument about money. Ben Franklin said there are two ways of solving money problems: augment your means—that is, make more money—or diminish your wants. Either will do. But the best plan of all is to do both at the same time. Think of ways to earn more money and diminish your wants. In this way, you'll live well within your means and always have a nice surplus of money.

WORRY

It's easier to win than to lose, and it's easier to succeed than to worry about failing. The reason most choose the latter is because it can be done sitting down.

We have more mental infirmities than all other illnesses combined. Dr. Charles H. Mayo once said that half the beds in the hospitals are filled by those people who worry themselves into them. You know, the mind is like an adding machine: before you can solve a problem with it, it must be cleared of all previous problems. Worry jams up the mechanism. It short-circuits the whole operation, impairing the most valuable mechanism on earth.

It's been proven many times that by a simple change in attitude and mental outlook, the same amount of time and energy devoted to worry could be used to solve our problems. Instead of worrying about the bills that have to be paid, shift gears and think creatively about ways of making more money. Instead of constantly stewing and fretting over a problem, we should try to think of ways of solving it.

Creative people look at problems as challenges. They realize that without problems everything would come to a stop. Problems are what keep the human race moving forward. Indeed, problems are responsible for every forward step we've ever taken—collectively or individually.

All industry exists solely for the solving of our problems, as does agriculture, education, and government. People go to school to learn to solve their problems or the problems of others. We've all got problems, and that's good. Without them, we'd still be swinging through the trees and living in caves.

And all problems are temporary. As the wise man said, "This too shall pass." So, if you want to have a lot more fun and a lot less worry, try to put your problems in perspective. See yourself as part of the world, and the world as part of the universe, and the universe as part of a great

And all problems are temporary. As the wise man said, "This too shall pass." So, if you want to have a lot more fun and a lot less worry, try to put your problems in perspective.

and mysterious living picture. Seen in their true light, most problems shrink to a modest size. Next, choose not to worry about them. Shift your mental gears. Clear your mind of worry and direct it to the solution of the problem at hand. It has a solution. It will be solved. The same kind of problems have been solved a million times before.

THREE GIFTS TO A NEWBORN CHILD

Bill Brewer was an especially astute interviewer and caught me completely off guard by his first question. He said, "If you could grant three qualities to a newborn child, what would they be?"

How would you like to be caught off guard early in the morning with that one? And for that matter, what would your answer be? "If you could grant three special qualities to a newborn child, what would they be?" I fed the question into my mental computer, thinking of my own children as I did, and I replied that I would grant the child, first, a consuming curiosity about everything—a love of knowledge. Second, I would grant the child a profound love for the earth and everything that lives upon it. And third, I would grant that child the gift of communication so that he or she could pass on to others what was learned during his or her lifetime.

Later, over breakfast, with more time to think about the question, I found I stuck with my original answers. How about you? What three gifts would you confer upon the child? Whatever they are, if your children are still young enough, or not yet born, you can pass them on to them.

With a love of learning, the person would never be bored nor find himself or herself stagnating at a certain level of accomplishment. The more we learn, the more we can do—and the more we venture to do, the more we learn. It's a self-generating perpetual motion kind of thing, for at least as long as we live. And with a deep love of learning, our person would develop a rich sense of humor, because as we learn more and more, the more we tend to pass through stultifying dogma and the lugubrious fearful threats preached by those who would keep us in bondage. Knowledge is freedom; freedom leads to joy and laughter. What was it Thucydides said? "The secret of happiness is freedom. And the secret of freedom is courage."

But with a love of the earth and all the living creatures on it, our person would have a deep sense of sympathy for anything or anyone in need. Our person would do whatever he or she could do to ameliorate suffering or the lack of personal freedom wherever it existed. Our person would be a natural champion of the environment but would understand that the environment is to be used and enjoyed as well as cared for and protected.

And as our person grew in maturity, he or she would most certainly be helping others to see the wonders and joys and problems of the world about us through one or more means of mass communication. Learning, loving, and communicating—not too bad, I should think. A lifetime of interest, love, and keeping in touch with life as we know it here on the planet Earth.

With those three qualities, our person would travel all over the earth and get to know this rather small speck of sand in the galaxy we call home and all the people and other living creatures that share it with us.

What are some of the qualities you value in yourself that were passed on to you?

What are the qualities you value in those closest to you?

Are these qualities you possess or would like to possess? How would they improve your life?

LEARNING TO SEE WITH THE SOUL

One of the major tragedies of growing up is that the majority of us lose that wonderful capacity of children to see emotionally. Do you remember how you saw things when you were a small child? Sometimes things—and quite often the simplest—seemed so beautiful to us it was almost unbearable. That's why a small child, still unspoiled by the acquisitiveness of modern society, will keep the box or wrapping paper and throw away the gift.

I was fortunate to live a part of my childhood on a small farm in Northern California. It was beautiful country, and I can remember how the earth smelled after a rain and how unutterably beautiful everything was: the trees, the grass, the poppies, the sky, the clouds, the birds, the puddles of water in the dirt road. Every walk in the fields or woods was the greatest kind of adventure filled with beauty.

Well, I was reading W. H. Hudson—probably the greatest naturalist of his time—and came across this line:

> We may say that the impressions are vivid and live vividly in the mind, even to the end of life, in those alone in whom something that is of the child survives in the adult—the measureless delight in all this visible world, experienced every day by the millions of children happily born outside the city's gates; and with the delight, the sense of wonder in all life, which is also akin to, if not one with, the mythical faculty, and if experienced in a high degree is a sense of the supernatural in all natural things. We may say, in fact, that unless the soul goes out to meet what we see, we do not see it; nothing do we see—not a beetle, not a blade of grass.

That's why two people can look at the same sight and while one is transformed and struck dumb by the awesome beauty of it, the other person will turn and walk away. And the fact is, the other person didn't see it. He looked, but he didn't see it.

I remember coming back from Europe by ship one time, and one morning I came on deck to see the most beautiful and magnificent island I had ever seen. It was São Miguel, in the eastern Azores. I stood at the rail transformed by its sudden beauty for several minutes, then rushed below to bring my wife and son to see it. They thought it was beautiful too, but I could tell they had not been affected by it as I had. In the case of something else, things could very likely be reversed. But when we see, as Hudson says, somehow with the soul, "unless the soul goes out to meet what we see, we do not see it."

What makes an artist great (a writer, painter, or musician) is that in his work he is able, through some transcendent magic, to make things so real to us we are able to see them in that way—with our souls going out to them. It's very difficult to express, but anyone who's been a child can usually remember the wonderful way things appeared. The trick and the idea is to keep that faculty alive.

SELF AND/OR GROUP CONVERSATION STARTERS

1. What is the cause of your stress? People— or your perception and interpretation of what someone brings to situations? Do your reactions usually make the circumstances better or worse?

2. What do you worry about the most? What did you think of the percentage statistics that were listed? Are finances a constant/sometimes/seldom worry?

3. What three gifts would you ideally confer upon a child? What three gifts would you realistically confer upon a child?

4. So you see yourself as part of the universe, part of a great and mysterious living picture? Can you clear your mind of worry and direct it to finding a solution to the problem? How are these two questions intertwined?

5. If you didn't answer the following questions while reading the chapter, do so now:

6. What are some of the qualities you value in yourself that were passed on to you?

7. What are the qualities you value in those closest to you?

8. Are these qualities you possess or would like to possess? How would they improve your life?

9. What do you understand as the meaning of the phrase, "unless the soul goes out to meet what we see, we do not see it"?

THE CALM OF LAUGHTER

There's a marriage counselor who has had a lot of success in saving marriages on the brink of dissolution by suggesting that whenever one of the partners starts an argument, the other partner should make him or her laugh. Real trouble begins when laughter goes out of a marriage.

One husband said, "How in the world can I get her to laugh? She hasn't laughed in three years."

"What made her laugh three years ago?" the counselor asked.

The husband thought for a moment and then said, "I fell on the ice in front of the house."

"Then you've got the answer. Whenever she starts an argument, fall down and make her laugh."

This made them both laugh, of course, and the doctor went on to suggest that the husband think of anything that might be silly enough to get them both laughing. "Stick celery in your ears...anything."

I remember many years ago we were rehearsing a dramatic radio series in Chicago, and the rehearsal had been going badly. The script wasn't the best; a couple of the actors and actresses weren't happy with their parts; the director was getting edgy; it was a cold, snowy day; and just as we were moodily about to try to do the dress rehearsal, since time was slipping away from us, one of the actors went out of the studio for a moment and returned suddenly with loud moans, staggering crazily, his eyes crossed and the ends of a pencil protruding from his ears.

He had broken a long yellow pencil in half and had stuck the broken ends into his ears. Grisly as the sign was, appearing as it did that someone had pushed a pencil through his head, it threw us all—the director, the engineers, the sound effects people, and the musicians—into fits of uncontrolled laughter until we were helpless with tears running down our faces. From that point on we were all right, and the show was one of the best we did that year.

Laughter is wonderfully therapeutic. If your kids get into an argument, give them each a cloth or paper towel and put them on opposite sides of the same window with instructions to clean it. No matter how angry they may have been, just looking through the glass at each other cleaning the window will soon have them howling with laughter, the argument forgotten.

There was a doctor who made it a practice to look for pictures in magazines and newspapers of people laughing—laughing hard. He cut them out and pasted them in a scrapbook. When the book was full, he took it to the hospital and let the nurses pass it around the wards. You can't look at other people laughing without laughing yourself, and the effect on the patients and nurses was wonderful.

Perhaps this is why good comedians are among the highest paid of the world's performers: people need to laugh. You can't feel worried or depressed when you're convulsed with laughter. It seems to have a beneficial effect on the human mind and organs. We're the only creatures on earth who can laugh—and the only ones with enough problems to need it.

I remember reading about a husband who, when he had a nerve-wracking day at the office, would come home with his hat on backwards. If his wife had a bad day, she'd wear her apron backwards. In either case, it would start them laughing and clearing the air.

A THERAPEUTIC SENSE OF HUMOR

In his book *Laughter & Liberation*, psychologist Harvey Mindess points out that everyone seems to realize the importance of a sense of humor. Indeed, the ability to see

A sense of humor helps us contend with adversity, derive greater joy out of living, and maintain our sanity.

the funny side of things and to laugh at ourselves and our troubles is an asset of the greatest magnitude. It can help us contend with adversity, derive greater joy out of living, and maintain our sanity. Yet no one seems to know how to cultivate a sense of humor.

The kind of humor that deserves to be called "therapeutic" is not the kind that enjoys jokes and comic routines. For as delightful as they may be, they are contrived and superficial, bearing about the same relation to therapeutic humor as pretty pictures do to real art. The kind of sense of humor that can help us maintain our sanity moves beyond jokes, beyond wit, and beyond laughter itself. It must constitute a frame of mind, a point of view, a far-reaching attitude toward life.

A cluster of qualities characterizes this peculiar frame of mind:

1. Flexibility – the willingness to examine every side of every issue (and every side of every side)

2. Spontaneity – the ability to leap from one mood or mode of thought to another

3. Unconventionality – freedom from the values of a person's place, time, and profession

4. Shrewdness – the refusal to believe that anyone, least of all himself or herself, is what they seem to be

5. Playfulness – the perspective that life is a tragic comic game that nobody wins but that does not have to be won to be enjoyed

6. Humility – that elusive quality whereby a person can shrug off the meaninglessness of his or her profoundest thoughts

These six qualities constitute the type of humor that everyone needs.

EIGHT WORDS TO LIVE BY

Ever since people have been able to communicate, they have compiled words to live by. But the world is still troubled. Take these words: honesty—workmanship—ambition—faith—education—charity—courage. Chances are 4.5 billion people won't agree to live their lives by them. But think how much better your life would be if just one person does. You.

With those eight words—eight concepts, really—you'd have about all the good advice you'd ever need to live a productive, rewarding, satisfying life. Let me go over the words once more.

Honesty: It means honesty in everything we do or say—honesty as a way of life. It's saying, "If it isn't honest, I won't have anything to do with it."

Workmanship: Workmanship is not a male or female word, even though it contains the word "man" in the middle of it. It means doing a job as well as we can do it without becoming neurotically obsessed with it. It's the kind of work one expects from a top professional. It's saying, "Everything I do, I will do to the best of my ability."

Ambition: Ambition is a good thing. It means moving toward something we believe to be worthwhile. Ambition keeps us on the most interesting of journeys. And as we'll find when we fulfill our ambition, the journey is better than the accomplishment. Ambition is the desire to do something, and human beings are at their best when they're doing things. Succeed at what you're now doing, and then move on to your next ambition.

As for the idea of *faith,* the fourth word in the list, we could talk about that all day. Faith makes everything work, and faith in ourselves and what we believe in is the driving power of our ambition.

And next comes *education*—a very big word that means many things. It's certainly not limited to schooling, although that's important, too. The better our education; the broader, the more comprehensive our knowledge; the better, the richer, the more interesting our lives become, and the more we'll understand the true meaning of the words we're discussing here today.

The next one is *charity,* which is a lot more than giving to the United Way, although that's part of it. It's having an attitude of charity; understanding that the more we share,

Courage turns the darkness into bright daylight, problems into possibilities.

the more we get, and the more we help and lift up others, the more we are helped and lifted up ourselves.

Responsibility means responsibility for ourselves and our lives. If something's wrong in our lives, chances are we're a big part of the problem.

And of course, *courage*. Courage turns the darkness into bright daylight, problems into possibilities.

CALMNESS

If ever there were a quality needed in the crisis-filled world today, it's calmness and the kind of clear thinking that calmness produces.

Remain calm. Attend to the day's challenges and opportunities with an even-tempered disposition, serenely and confidently approaching each task with the knowledge of and commitment to your course. I wonder how improved our days would be if we would make a point of going over that little message every morning.

Here's something that we should read once a day for the next 45 years. It was written back at the turn of the century by William George Jordan. He was editor of several magazines during his lifetime, including the *Ladies Home Journal* and *The Saturday Evening Post*.

He wrote:

Calmness is the rarest quality in human life. It is the poise of a great nature, in harmony with itself and its ideals. It is the moral atmosphere of a life self-reliant and self-controlled. Calmness is singleness of purpose, absolute confidence, and conscious power ready to be focused in an instant to meet any crisis.

The Sphinx is not a true type of calmness. Petrification is not calmness; it's death—the silencing of all the energies. While no one lives his life more fully, more intentionally, and more consciously than the person who's calm, the fatalist is not calm. He's the coward's slave of his environment, hopelessly surrendering to his present condition, recklessly indifferent to his future. He accepts his life as a rudderless ship drifting on the ocean of time. He has no compass, no chart, no known port to which he is sailing. His self-confessed inferiority to all nature is shown in his existence of constant surrender. It is not calmness.

The person who is calm has his course in life clearly marked on his chart. His hand is ever on the helm. Storm, fog, night, tempest, danger, hidden reefs—he's prepared and ready for them. He's made calm and serene by the realization that in these crises of his voyage, he needs a clear mind and a cool head, then he has nothing to do but do each day the best he can by the light he has; that he will never

If ever there were
a quality needed in
the crisis-filled world
today, it's calmness
and the kind of
clear thinking that
calmness produces.

flinch or falter for a moment; that though he may have to tack and leave his course for a time, he'll keep ever headed toward his harbor. When he will reach it, how he will reach it, matters not to him. He rests in calmness knowing he did his best.

When the worries and cares of the day fret you and begin to wear upon you and you chafe under the friction, be calm. Stop. Rest for a moment, and let calmness and peace assert themselves. If you let these irritating outside influences get the better of you, you're confessing your inferiority to them by permitting them to dominate you. When the tongue of malice and slander, the persecution of inferiority, tempt you to retaliate; when for an instant you forget yourself so far as to hunger for revenge, be calm. When the grey heron is pursued by its enemy, the eagle, it does not run to escape. It remains calm, takes a dignified stand, and waits quietly, facing the enemy unmoved. With a terrific force with which the eagle makes its attack, the boasted king of birds is often impaled and run through on the quiet, lance-like bill of the heron. No person in the world ever attempted to wrong another without being injured in return some way, somehow, some time. Remain calm.

Now all of that was written at the turn of the century and in language that today might sound a bit affected and archaic. It's a good message. If ever there were a quality needed in the crisis-filled world of today, it's calmness—and the kind of clear thinking calmness produces.

I wonder how improved our days would be if we would make it a point to go over that little message every morning.

SELF AND/OR GROUP CONVERSATION STARTERS

1. Which of the examples, if any, at the beginning of the chapter caused you to laugh out loud, or at least smile? Did the examples give you ideas about how you can diffuse the next tense situation?

2. Of the six qualities that constitute the type of humor that everyone needs, which have you mastered? Which are you still working on?

3. Considering the eight words to live by listed, how many additional words would you add that would make the list more complete from your perspective? List those words and the reason why you would include them.

4. Do you routinely go about the day's challenges and opportunities with an even-tempered disposition, serenely and confidently approaching each task with the knowledge of and commitment to its successful completion?

5. *"Courage* turns the darkness into bright daylight, problems into possibilities." Considering that generalized definition of courage, think of a current situation where you exhibited courage and write your own definition.

6. "Calmness is singleness of purpose, absolute confidence, and conscious power ready to be focused in an instant to meet any crisis." Does this quote accurately describe you? Do you wish it did? What will you do to make it so?

EARL
NIGHTINGALE'S
30-DAY
CHALLENGE

A human being must have something worthwhile toward which he's working.

Nightingale's famous thirty-day test has transformed the mindsets—*and lives*—of countless people across the globe, giving them phenomenal levels of financial and professional success, as well as the ultimate form of wealth—an abiding, deep-rooted *joy of life.*

Now it's your turn to implement this life-changing challenge. In thirty days, you will discover more abundance than you could ever have imagined—likely monetary riches, but more importantly, emotional riches like serenity, satisfaction, and gratitude. While the test lasts only a month, it should be repeated again and again until it becomes a part of you.

Nightingale's challenge addresses two facets of the human condition: our core desires as well as our basic fears. As he says, "Each of us wants something, and each of us is afraid of something." This reality undergirds his philosophy of individual achievement, which is grounded in the science of the mind—namely, the notion that thoughts are things, and when you change your thoughts, you change your reality.

Accordingly, the thirty-day test recommends actions that will turn your innermost desire into a concrete goal and your nagging fears into a new, productive habit. It involves two ongoing processes:

GOAL-MAKING

- Write on a card what it is you want more than anything else—a single, clearly defined goal.

- On the other side, write the following lines from the Sermon on the Mount:

Ask, and it shall be given you; seek, and ye shall find; knock, and it shall be opened unto you. For every one that asketh receiveth; and he that seeketh findeth; and to him that knocketh it shall be opened.

—Matthew 7:7–8 KJV

- Carry this card with you at all times, and periodically take it out and read both sides. Make sure to remain positive about your goal. As Nightingale instructs, "Think about it in a cheerful, relaxed way." He further advises: "As you look at it, remember that you must become what you think about, and since you're thinking about your goal, you realize that soon it will be yours."

NEW HABIT FORMATION

- The second component of the test involves refraining from thinking about your fears— because the rule that "you become what you think about" applies just as much to negative thoughts as it does to positive ones.

- Nightingale instructs: "Each time a fearful or negative thought comes into your consciousness, replace it with a mental picture of your positive and worthwhile goal."

These two activities—remaining focused on your most desired goal and not succumbing to intrusive negative thoughts—are inherently intertwined. The idea is to maintain a cheerful, relaxed, positive outlook on life while intensively pursuing your dreams. Doing so will not only ensure that you reach your goals; it will also guarantee your enjoyment of the process—because as Nightingale repeatedly emphasizes throughout his work, having goals are what give life meaning.

His first rule of living is that "a human being must have something worthwhile toward which he's working. Without that, everything else—even the most remarkable achievements and all the trappings of worldly success— tend to turn sour." Nightingale adds: "The moment you decide on a goal to work toward, you're immediately a successful person." For him, the journey of pursuing your

The moment you decide on a goal to work toward, you're immediately a successful person.

goals is just as important, if not more important, than the attainment of them. And riches can be found in both the process and the product.

In addition to maintaining a cheerful, positive outlook while reflecting on and taking action to reach your goal, Nightingale recommends giving of yourself more than you've ever done before. Work harder at your job than you ever have. Take on extra tasks with a positive attitude, and do your regular duties with a keener eye for detail and commitment to excellence than usual. Add value before expecting returns to manifest, and value will be added unto you. The law of giving and receiving, of sowing and reaping, ensures that you will receive in equal measure that which you contribute: poison for poison, or bounty for bounty; failure for toxic, negative thoughts, or success for positive, peaceful thoughts. In other words, emit thoughts with positive frequencies that will yield a generous harvest of riches.

Note that if at any point in the thirty days, you vocalize a negative thought, you must start over again from that point and go thirty more days.

STARTING YOUR
30-DAY TEST

In order to begin your thirty-day challenge, you must decide upon a concrete goal to pursue. Nightingale recommends that you choose only one to focus on for this particular test, so you'll have to identify your most desired objective.

Nightingale provides the following questions to help you determine what it is you truly want in life:

1. If you could completely change places with any other person in the world, would you do it, and who would that person be?

_____

_____

_____

_____

_____

2. If you could work at any job, would that work be different from the work you're doing now?

_____

_____

_____

_____

_____

_____

3. If you could live in any part of the country, would you move from where you're now living, and if so, where?

_____

_____

_____

_____

4. If you could go back to age twelve and live your life from that point over again, would you do it? And what would you do differently?

_____

_____

_____

_____

Nightingale notes that most people will answer "no" to all four questions, even when they're generally dissatisfied with their present lives—which, in his mind, explains their unhappiness. For goals are what give our lives purpose and direction.

Go ahead and think critically upon each one of these questions. Journal about your responses, exploring not only the *who, what, where,* and *how* questions implied in prompts 1–4, but also the *whys*:

5. If you would change places with someone, why that particular person? What is it about his or her life that you would like to emulate? Can you identify in one sentence, or even one phrase, what that person has that you desire?

_____

_____

_____

_____

_____

_____

6. If you would choose a different profession, why that specific career? What qualities about that career make it desirable to you? Are any of these qualities present in your current job that could be further developed? What is your most desired job title and why?

_____

_____

_____

_____

_____

_____

_____

7. If you would like to move to a different location, why that particular location? What aspects of that location make it ideal for your home? Are any of these qualities present in other locations, including your current one? Or, do you simply desire a different home in the same general location?

_____

_____

_____

_____

_____

_____

_____

_____

_____

_____

_____

_____

_____

_____

_____

_____

_____

_____

8. Why would doing that particular thing in your life over again differently make a difference? What was it about that action or event that you didn't like? What were its consequences? Why would the alternate scenario you imagined in the above prompt have produced better results?

_____

_____

_____

_____

_____

_____

_____

_____

_____

_____

_____

_____

_____

_____

_____

_____

Based on your answers to these questions, rank, on a scale of 1 to 6 (1 being most desired and 6 being least desired), the areas of your life in which you most desire change:

- [ ] Wellness
- [ ] Finances
- [ ] Career
- [ ] Location
- [ ] Personality
- [ ] Relationships

After selecting the department of living upon which you'll focus your thirty-day test from the list above, find the correlating prompt below to help write your concrete goal statement on the front side of your reminder card.

Remember, your goal statement should be **one concise sentence** that clearly defines a **specific** goal. Use one or more of the questions in the category of your choice to formulate your unique goal statement.

WELLNESS

1. How do you define "health" or "wellness"?

_____
_____
_____
_____
_____
_____
_____

2. If you imagine yourself living at a peak level of wellness, what does that involve?

_____
_____
_____
_____
_____
_____
_____
_____

3. How does your current lifestyle
differ from the lifestyle required for
your ideal state of wellness?

_____

_____

_____

_____

_____

_____

_____

_____

4. What are you willing to sacrifice
to reach your wellness goal?

_____

_____

_____

_____

_____

_____

_____

_____

Sample Goal Statements

I desire increased health/wellness in my life, which
entails _____.

In _____ [years/months], I would like to _____
[lose _____ pounds; take up _____ sport or
mindfulness regimen; transition into veganism; etc.].

_____

_____

_____

_____

_____

_____

_____

_____

_____

_____

_____

_____

_____

_____

FINANCES

1. What is the salary that would make you content, comfortable, or overjoyed? Write an exact number.

_____

2. Do you have any debt that you would like cleared? How much does this debt amount to? In how many years would you like to pay off this balance? How will you feel when you clear this debt?

_____
_____
_____
_____
_____
_____
_____
_____
_____
_____
_____

3. How much money would you like to contribute to savings each month? Or what other investments would you like to make?

_____
_____
_____
_____
_____
_____
_____
_____
_____
_____
_____
_____

4. What large item would you like to purchase? How much is required for you to purchase this item?

_____
_____
_____
_____

5. How much money would you like to give annually or monthly to philanthropic purposes? To what causes would you contribute your funds? Why do you value these causes?

_____

_____

_____

_____

_____

_____

_____

6. What are you willing to give up to reach your financial goal?

_____

_____

_____

_____

_____

_____

_____

Sample Goal Statements

In ____ years, I would like to make _____ and be able to contribute _____ annually to charities like _____ and _____.

In ____ years, I would like to pay off _____ in debt and be making _____ per year.

I will forgo _____ [miscellaneous expense] in order to save an extra _____ per month.

I will save _____ each month in order to buy _____ in _____ [years/months].

_____

_____

_____

_____

_____

_____

_____

_____

CAREER

1. What is your dream job and why? Include the specific job title in your description.

_____

_____

_____

_____

_____

_____

2. Is there a different role in your current company that you would rather have? If so, what? Write the specific job title.

_____

_____

_____

_____

_____

_____

_____

3. Do you desire to start your own business? If so, what kind? Why do you value entrepreneurship?

_____

_____

_____

_____

_____

_____

_____

4. If your dream job is in a different field than your current one, what education or training will be required for you to change professions? Or who could mentor you in your desired industry?

_____

_____

_____

_____

_____

_____

_____

5. In how many years would you like
to make this job change?

_____

_____

6. What are you willing to sacrifice to
reach your professional goal?

_____

_____

_____

_____

_____

_____

_____

_____

_____

_____

_____

_____

_____

_____

_____

Sample Goal Statements

In ____ years, I would like to be the

_____ at my current company.

In ____ years, I would like to start my own

_____ company because

_____.

In ____ years, I would like to switch professions to

_____, which means that I'll need to seek

training in _____.

_____

_____

_____

_____

_____

_____

_____

_____

_____

_____

_____

LOCATION

1. Where in the world would you most like to live and why?

_____

_____

_____

_____

_____

_____

_____

2. Can you do your current job in this location, or would you need to change careers? What else would be required to move to this other place?

_____

_____

_____

_____

_____

_____

_____

_____

3. In what type of home would you most like to live? Describe the specific home type (Cape Cod, colonial, craftsman, etc.; two-story, ranch, split-level, etc.; brick, stucco, etc.) in as much detail as possible.

_____

_____

_____

_____

_____

_____

_____

_____

4. What are you willing to give up to live in this location?

_____

_____

_____

_____

_____

_____

_____

Sample Goal Statements

In ____ [years/months], I would like to live in

_____ .

In ____ [years/months], I will move into a ____ style house in _____ [location].

_____

_____

_____

_____

_____

_____

_____

_____

_____

_____

_____

_____

_____

_____

_____

_____

PERSONALITY

1. What are the qualities in other people I most like? Which of these qualities could I do better to cultivate?

_____

_____

_____

2. What personality characteristics would most lend themselves to a happier, more cheerful, more relaxed life?

_____

_____

_____

3. What am I willing to change about my current life to adopt a more pleasing (both to self and to others) personality?

_____

_____

_____

Sample Goal Statements

I intend to become a better version of myself, which involves cultivating the following personality characteristics:

_____

_____

_____

_____

_____

_____

_____

_____

_____

_____

_____

_____

_____

_____

_____

Every day, I will remain calm, positive, and grateful, approaching each challenge as an opportunity for growth and success.

RELATIONSHIPS

1. How could my current relationships be improved?

_____

_____

_____

_____

_____

_____

_____

_____

2. What relationships are currently absent from my life that I would like to cultivate?

_____

_____

_____

_____

_____

_____

_____

_____

3. What am I willing to sacrifice to develop, repair, or improve these relationships?

_____

_____

_____

_____

_____

_____

— Sample Goal Statements —

In ____ [years/months], I will find my future [spouse/partner] by _____ .

In ____ [years/months], I will strengthen my relationship with _____ , which will require _____ .

_____

_____

_____

_____

_____

_____

ABOUT EARL NIGHTINGALE

Earl **Nightingale** (1921-1989) was a man of many talents and interests—nationally syndicated radio personality, entrepreneur, philosopher, US Marine, and others. One thread united all his pursuits—a passion for excellence and living a meaningful existence.

Earl Nightingale's life began simply. He grew up in Long Beach, California. His parents had little money, and his father disappeared when he was 12. But even as a boy, Earl was always asking questions, always reading in his local public library, trying to understand the way life works.

Stationed aboard the battleship, USS Arizona, he was one of a handful of survivors when that ship was destroyed and sank at Pearl Harbor. After being separated from the Marine Corps, and starting with practically nothing, in ten years he founded and headed four corporations. He wrote, sold, and produced fifteen radio and television programs per week.

Nightingale appeared on all major networks and for four years was the star of the dramatic series *Sky King*, which was carried on more than 500 stations of the Mutual Radio Network. He also began an insurance agency and in twelve months led it from last to sixth place in the nation with one of the world's largest companies.

The Nation's Press carried the astounding story of the phenomenally successful young man who, at 35, had become financially independent. He produced his famous recording of *The Strangest Secret*, revealing how anyone can make the most of his or her own capabilities and can attain a rich full measure of success and happiness, right in his or her present job or position. Its theme: "How to achieve greater success and enjoy greater happiness and peace of mind."

At the time, this inspiring recording broke records, selling in the multimillions to major industries, retailers and salespeople, clubs and associations, parents, students, and people in virtually all walks of life. His masterful recording has been adapted into a book and videos.